HOUGHTON MIFFLIN HARCOURT

WRITE SOURCE

SkillsBook

TEACHER'S EDITION

Grade 2

GREAT
SOURCE.

 HOUGHTON MIFFLIN HARCOURT

A Few Words About the *Write Source SkillsBook* **Grade 2**

Before you begin . . .

The *SkillsBook* provides you with opportunities to practice editing and proofreading skills presented in *Write Source*. *Write Source* contains guidelines, examples, and models to help you complete your work in the *SkillsBook*.

Each *SkillsBook* activity includes a brief introduction to the topic and examples showing how to complete that activity. You will be directed to the page numbers in *Write Source* for additional information and examples.

The "Proofreading Activities" focus on punctuation, capitalization, spelling, and usage. The "Sentence Activities" help you understand sentences and common sentence problems. The "Language Activities" highlight the parts of speech.

Many exercises end with a **KEEP GOING** activity. Its purpose is to provide follow-up work that will help you apply what you have learned in your own writing.

Copyright © by Houghton Mifflin Harcourt Publishing Company

Printed in the U.S.A.

ISBN   978-0-547-48433-4

3 4 5 6 7 8 9 10 0928 17 16 15 14 13 12

4500357637   A B C D E F G

Table of Contents

Proofreading Activities

Using Punctuation

Checking Mechanics

Using the Right Word

Sentence Activities

Language Activities

Proofreading Activities

The activities in this section include sentences that need to be checked for mechanics or usage. Most of the activities also include helpful *Write Source* references. In addition, KEEP GOING, which is at the end of many activities, encourages follow-up practice of certain skills.

Name _____

Periods as End Punctuation

A **period** is used as a signal to stop at the end of a sentence. Put a period at the end of a telling sentence.

  A   **Put periods at the ends of these telling sentences.**

1. Our class lines up at the main door ____•____

2. Sometimes we make our teacher smile ____•____

3. We play indoors on rainy days ____•____

4. There are some great new books in the library ____•____

5. I like to write funny stories ____•____

  B   **Write two telling sentences about your school.**

1. _____

_____

2. _____

_____

C Put a period at the end of each sentence in this letter.

October 10, 2011

Dear Aunt Fran,

I like school this year. There are 22 kids in my class. A new boy sits next to me. His name is Robert. I think we're going to be friends. I'll let you know in my next letter.

Love,

Timmy

Now answer these questions about the letter.

1. How many telling sentences are in the letter? _____6_____

2. How many periods are in the letter? _____6_____

Name _____

Periods After Abbreviations

Use **periods** after these abbreviations:
Mr., Mrs., Ms., and Dr.

Dr. Green   Mrs. Linn

(**Dr.** is the abbreviation for **doctor**.)

A Put periods after the abbreviations in these sentences. (Some sentences need more than one period.)

1. Mrs. Linn is our teacher.

2. Mr. and Mrs. Linn have three rabbits.

3. Mr. Linn gave the rabbits their names.

4. They are Ms. Hop, Mr. Skip, and Mrs. Jump.

5. Mrs. Linn took the rabbits to Dr. Green for shots.

6. Dr. Green said, "Those are good names!"

7. Mrs. Linn told Dr. Green that Mr. Linn made up the names.

6

6

B Write two names for rabbits. One name should start with Mr. and one with Mrs. Then write two sentences that use the names.

Name: _Mr._____

Name: _Mrs._____

1. _____

_____

_____

2. _____

_____

_____

C Write the names of four grown-ups. Be sure to write Mr., Mrs., Ms., or Dr. before each name.

1. _____

2. _____

3. _____

4. _____

Name _____

Question Marks

Put a **question mark** after a
sentence that asks a question.

What is the longest river?

 A   Put a question mark after each sentence
that asks a question. Put a period after
each of the other sentences.

1. The world's longest river is the Nile __•__

2. Where is the Nile __?__

3. The Nile River is in Africa __•__

4. Are there crocodiles in the Nile __?__

5. You could jump in and find out __•__

6. Are you kidding __?__

7. I'd rather just ask someone __•__

8. Are you afraid of crocodiles __?__

9. Who wouldn't be afraid __?__

B Put a period or a question mark at the end of each sentence in this paragraph.

Lots of animals live in rivers. Of course, fish live in rivers. What else lives in rivers? Snails, frogs, and turtles live in and around rivers. Have you heard of river otters? They are very good at diving. They can stay underwater for four minutes. Do you know any other animals that live in rivers?

Write two questions about rivers. Remember to use question marks!

1. _____

_____

2. _____

_____

Name _____

Exclamation Points

Put an **exclamation point** after an *excited* word. Also put an exclamation point after a sentence showing strong feeling.

Help!   Yikes!

Don't touch that!

> **A** Use an exclamation point or period to finish each sentence. Remember, an exclamation point is used after each *excited* word and after each sentence that shows strong feeling. Telling sentences need a period.

1. I found a treasure map__!__

2. It was in my closet__.__

3. I found the map when I cleaned my room__.__

4. Wow__!__

5. Let's find the treasure__!__

6. We should ask our parents before we look__.__

7. This could be fun__!__

B Each of the following sentences needs an exclamation point or a question mark. Put the correct end punctuation after each sentence.

1. Look, Tom, it's a cave _____ !

2. It's dark _____ !

3. It's creepy _____ !

4. Did you see that _____ ?

5. What is it _____ ?

6. It's a bat _____ !

7. Wow, that's neat _____ !

8. Here we go _____ !

Imagine that you are in a dark cave. Write a sentence that ends with an exclamation point.

_____

_____

Name _____

End Punctuation

Use a **period** (.) after a telling sentence. Use a **question mark** (?) after a sentence that asks a question. Use an **exclamation point** (!) after a sentence that shows strong feeling.

A Put the correct end punctuation after each sentence.

(Some answers may vary.)

1. Dad's taking us to the zoo ___!___

2. Hooray! Let's have a race to the car ___!___

3. What animal does Dad like ___?___

4. He likes the elephants ___.___

5. What do you think Mom wants to see ___?___

6. She'll probably watch the giraffes ___.___

7. What should we do ___?___

8. Let's go see the seals ___! (or) •___

B Write a telling sentence, an asking sentence, and a sentence showing strong feeling about your favorite dinner.

Telling Sentence: _____

_____

Asking Sentence: _____

_____

Strong Feeling Sentence: _____

_____

C Ask a partner a question. Write your partner's name, the question you asked, and your partner's answer.

Partner's Name: _____

Question: _____

_____

Answer: _____

_____

Name _____

End Punctuation Review

Use a **period** after a telling sentence. Use a **question mark** after a sentence that asks a question. Use an **exclamation point** after a sentence that shows strong feeling.

 Put the correct end punctuation after each sentence.

(Some answers will vary.)

Does this ever happen to you? It's time for bed, but you're not sleepy. You try to lie still. You look around. You just have to get up! You want to get a book or a toy. You try to be quiet. It's hard to see in the dark! You make a loud noise. Someone says, "What's going on in there?" Then you hear, "Get back in bed!"

B Draw a picture of something you like to do after school.

C Write three sentences about your picture. First write a telling sentence. Next write a question. Then write a sentence that shows strong feeling.

1. Telling Sentence:_____

_____

2. Asking Sentence:_____

_____

3. Strong Feeling Sentence:_____

_____

Name _____

Commas Between Words in a Series

Put **commas** between words in a series.

The five senses are sight, hearing, taste, smell, and touch.

A Put commas where they are needed in these sentences.

1. Most foods taste sweet, sour, or salty.

2. Smell, sight, and taste help us enjoy food.

3. Almost everybody likes warm bread, biscuits, and dinner rolls.

4. Lilies, lilacs, and roses smell good.

5. Cats can see only black, white, and gray.

6. Dogs, cats, and bats hear all kinds of sounds.

7. Sounds can be loud, soft, or just right.

8. Teddy bears are soft, cuddly, and fuzzy.

16

B List three or four things in each category below.

My Favorite Tastes	My Favorite Smells	My Favorite Sounds

C Finish the sentences below using words from your lists. Remember to use commas between words in a series.

1. My favorite tastes are _____

_____ and _____ .

2. My favorite smells are _____

_____ and _____ .

3. My favorite sounds are _____

_____ and _____ .

Name _____

Commas in Compound Sentences

A **compound sentence** is two short sentences connected by *or*, *and*, or *but*. Always use a **comma** before the connecting word.

I have a goldfish, **and** I feed it once a day.

 A Add a comma to each of these compound sentences.

1. I love hamburgers, but I do not like onions.

2. My brother is three, and he goes to preschool.

3. You can walk, or you can ride your bike.

4. Dad came to the concert, but Mom had to work.

5. Our teacher is nice, and she loves dogs.

6. Sara will play the piano, or she will sing.

7. I asked Lee to play ball, but he was busy.

18

B Write compound sentences using the pairs of sentences below. Use the connecting word in parentheses to complete each sentence. Remember to add commas!

Do you see the bees? Can you hear them? (or)
Do you see the bees, or can you hear them?

1. Bees are busy. They all have jobs to do. *(and)*

Bees are busy, and they all have jobs to do.

_____

_____

2. Most bees work. The queen bee does not work. *(but)*

Most bees work, but the queen bee does not work.

_____

_____

3. Bees care for the queen. They make honey. *(or)*

Bees care for the queen, or they make honey.

_____

_____

Name _____

Commas to Set Off a Speaker's Words

When you write a speaker's exact words, you may tell who is speaking at the **beginning** of the sentence, or at the **end** of the sentence. Use a comma to set off the speaker's words, as shown below.

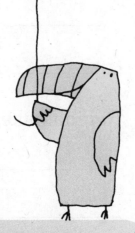

Mr. Kent said, "Kari, you may begin your report."

"My report is on birds," Kari said.

 A   **Put commas where they are needed in these sentences.**

"Many birds migrate in the winter," Kari said.

Darrin asked, "What does *migrate* mean?"

"Migrate means that some birds go to a new place in winter," Kari answered. She added, "Birds migrate to find food and water."

"That's very interesting," said Mr. Kent.

B Write questions that Bill and Regina might ask about birds and migration. Use question marks and commas correctly.

Bill asked __ " _____

_____

_____ "

Regina asked __ " _____

_____

_____ "

Write a question using a speaker's exact words. Include the speaker's name. Use quotation marks and a comma to set off the speaker's words.

_____

_____

_____

Name

Comma Between a City and a State

Put a **comma** between the name of a city and a state.

Austin, Texas   Salem, Oregon

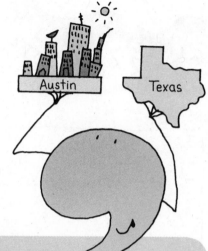

A Put commas between the cities and states below.

1. Calumet, Michigan

2. Casper, Wyoming

3. Williamsburg, Virginia

4. Portland, Maine

5. Dallas, Texas

6. Dayton, Ohio

B Write the name of the city and state shown on page 408 in your *Write Source*. Then write the name of another city and its state. Put a comma between the city and state.

1. _____

2. _____

22

 **Draw a picture of a place in your city or town. Beneath your drawing, write sentences about your picture.**

I live in _____

_____

_____

_____

_____

Name _____

Comma Between the Day and the Year

Put a **comma** between the day and the year.

January 17, 2011
November 12, 2011

October 2011

S	M	T	W	T	F	S
						1
2	3	4	5	6	7	8
9	10	⑪	12	13	14	15
16	17	18	19	20	21	22
23 30	24 31	25	26	27	28	29

A Look at the calendar on this page. Then write the correct month, day, and year.

1. Write the date that is circled.

October 11, 2011
_____

2. Write the date that has a diamond around it.

October 24, 2011
_____

3. Write the date for the last day of the month.

October 31, 2011
_____

4. Write the date for the first Wednesday of the month.

October 5, 2011
_____

B Write the dates for the following days. Be sure to include the month, day, and year. The months are listed on page 426 in *Write Source*.

1. Your next birthday:

_____

2. Today:

_____

3. Tomorrow:

_____

Write a true or make-believe sentence about the day you were born. Include the date of your birth in your sentence.

_____

_____

_____

_____

Name _____

Commas in Letters

Put **commas** after the greeting or salutation and the closing of a letter.

Dear Grandpa Joe, ← **greeting or salutation**
    I love my new fishing rod! Thank you!
Can we go fishing soon? I hope so!

              Love,
              Ben ↖ **closing**

 A   **Put commas where they belong in these letters.**

May 10, 2011
Dear Ben,
    Ask your mom
when your family is
coming to Florida.
Then we can go
fishing.
    Love,
    Grandpa Joe

May 18, 2011
Dear Grandpa Joe,
    We are coming to
see you on December
23rd. I can't wait!
My tackle box is
ready.
    Love,
    Ben

26

 **B** Put commas in Grandpa's letter. Then pretend you are Ben. Write what you would say in your next letter to Grandpa Joe. Be sure to put commas in the right places.

November 24, 2011

Dear Ben,
    I will be seeing you in one month! We'll camp out in a tent. We'll have a campfire.
        Love,
        Grandpa Joe

_____
(Date)

_____
(Greeting or Salutation)

_____

_____

_____
(Closing)

_____
(Signature)

© Houghton Mifflin Harcourt Publishing Company

Name
_____

Comma Review

This activity reviews comma uses you have learned.

 Put a comma between the names of the cities and the states in these sentences.

1. You can see mountains from Portland, Oregon.

2. The James River goes through Richmond, Virginia.

3. El Paso, Texas, is near Mexico.

4. Sitka, Alaska, is on the Pacific Ocean.

5. Hilo, Hawaii, is part of an island.

 Put a comma between the day and the year in these sentences.

1. George Washington was born February 22, 1732.

2. The first nickel was made on May 16, 1866.

3. On February 7, 1867, Laura Ingalls Wilder was born.

4. The astronaut Sally Ride was born May 26, 1951.

28

Put commas between words in a series in these sentences.

1. Red, orange, yellow, and green are rainbow colors.

2. My uncle, aunt, and cousin live in Michigan.

3. Jonathan likes snowboarding, sledding, and skiing.

4. My family has two cats, one dog, and a turtle.

5. I send letters, notes, and e-mail messages.

Put commas where they are needed.

Maggie asked, "What kind of seashell is that?"

"It's a heart cockle," Molly said. "If you put two together, they form a heart."

"Amazing!" Maggie added. "What's this one?"

"It's called a turkey wing," Molly answered.

"That's a perfect name! It looks just like one," said Maggie.

Name _____

Making Contractions 1

A **contraction** turns two words into one word. To make a contraction, put an **apostrophe** where one or more letters are left out.

Two Words	Contraction
does not	doesn't
we have	we've

 A In the second column, cross out the letters that are left out of the contraction in the first column.

Contraction	Two Words
1. I'm	I am
2. she'll	she will
3. he's	he is
4. they're	they are
5. he'd	he would
6. hasn't	has not
7. we'll	we will
8. shouldn't	should not

30

B Make contractions from the words below.
Remember to use an apostrophe each time!

1. do not _____don't_____

2. that is _____that's_____

3. cannot _____can't_____

4. I have _____I've_____

C On each blank below, write the contraction for the words in parentheses.

1. _____I'm_____ going to make a mask.
     (I am)

2. _____I'll_____ make it out of a paper bag.
     (I will)

3. _____It's_____ going to be a scary mask.
     (It is)

4. Dad _____doesn't_____ know I am making it.
       (does not)

Name

Making Contractions 2

A **contraction** turns two words into one word. To make a contraction, put an **apostrophe** where one or more letters are left out.

Two Words   **Contraction**

she will   she'll

A   In each sentence, underline the contraction. Then write the word or words the contraction stands for.

1. "Peter didn't obey Mom," said Flopsy. ___did not___

2. "You can't go to the ball," she told Cinderella.

   ___cannot___

3. "You wouldn't help me," said the Little Red Hen.

   ___would not___

4. "I couldn't sleep in that bumpy bed," said the princess.

   ___could not___

5. The wolf said, "I'll blow your house down." ___I will___

6. "I'm a real boy!" shouted Pinocchio. ___I am___

B **Write the two words that each contraction stands for.**

1. doesn't _____does not_____

2. hasn't _____has not_____

3. he's _____he is_____

4. I've _____I have_____

5. isn't _____is not_____

6. it's _____it is_____

7. we're _____we are_____

8. you'll _____you will_____

Write a sentence using one of the contractions above.

_____

_____

_____

Name

Apostrophes to Show Ownership 1

Add an **apostrophe** and an *s* to a word to show ownership.

Tom has a boat.   It is Tom's boat.

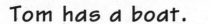

A   Each phrase below shows ownership. Draw a picture in each box.

the cat's rug	the bird's nest
Susan's jump rope	my mother's hat

B Write the words below to show ownership. Be sure to add an apostrophe and an *s* to each word.

1. the _____tree's_____ leaves
   (tree)

2. the _____kite's_____ string
   (kite)

3. the _____airplane's_____ wing
   (airplane)

4. the _____bird's_____ tail
   (bird)

C Write the names below to show ownership. Add an apostrophe and an *s* to each name.

1. I see _____Maria's_____ purple pencil.
   (Maria)

2. This is _____Don's_____ math book.
   (Don)

3. _____Jane's_____ backpack is heavier than mine.
   (Jane)

4. _____Sol's_____ idea notebook is on the desk.
   (Sol)

Name

Apostrophes to Show Ownership 2

Add an **apostrophe** and an *s* to a word to show ownership.

The cat's tail is white.

The cat's whiskers are white, too.

 A Add an apostrophe in each sentence to show ownership.

1. Molly's cat is named Ink because he has black fur.

2. Robert's new kitten is as white as snow.

3. His cat's name is Marshmallow.

4. Marshmallow's fur looks brown after she plays in the garden.

5. Jennifer's brown cat is named Cocoa.

6. Cocoa's fur always stays brown, wherever she plays.

B Put apostrophes where needed to show ownership in this letter.

November 11, 2010

Dear Uncle Frank,

I can hardly wait for Father's Day. Dad's friend Fernando is coming over. Fernando's stories about growing up in Brazil are amazing. Plus, he likes Nicky's funny stories. Mom's one wish is that her brother Frank could come!

Love,

Sam

Now answer this question about the letter.

1. How many apostrophes did you add? _____5_____

Name _____

Underlining Titles

Underline the titles of books and magazines.

a book — <u>Onion Sundaes</u>

a magazine — <u>3, 2, 1 Contact</u>

A **Underline the titles in the following sentences.**

1. My sister's favorite book is <u>Pocahontas</u>.

2. My grandmother has a book called <u>Mrs. Bird</u>.

3. <u>Kids Discover</u> is a magazine for kids.

4. The title of our book is <u>Write Source</u>.

5. <u>Ranger Rick</u> is a nature magazine for kids.

6. I just read <u>Ira Sleeps Over</u> by Bernard Waber.

7. My dad reads <u>National Geographic</u> every month.

8. Our teacher is reading <u>All About Sam</u> to us.

B **Complete the following sentences. Remember to underline the titles.**

1. My favorite book is _____

_____.

2. My favorite magazine is _____

_____.

3. The title of the last book I read is _____

_____.

Draw a cover for one of your favorite books. Write the book title on your cover.

Name _____

Quotation Marks Before and After a Speaker's Words

Comic strips make it easy to tell who is speaking. They use speech balloons. Here Mom and Steve are talking about dinner.

Mom,
may we make
pizza for dinner?

That sounds
really good
to me.

PIZZA
MIX

When you write sentences, you use **quotation marks** to show the speaker's exact words.

Steve asked, "Mom, may we make pizza for dinner?"

"That sounds really good to me," Mom said.

 **Read the speech balloons. Then write the sentences below. Put quotation marks where they are needed.**

May we make pepperoni pizza?

Yes. Let's add something else.

Steve asked, "May we make pepperoni pizza?"

_____

Mom answered, "Yes. Let's add something else."

_____

How about mushrooms?

Great choice!

Steve asked, "How about mushrooms?"

_____

Mom said, "Great choice!"

_____

Name _____

Punctuation Review

This review covers punctuation marks you have learned.

 **Fill in each list below.**

Cat Names	City Names	Food Names
1. Buddy	1. _____	1. _____
2. _____	2. _____	2. _____
3. _____	3. _____	3. _____

B **Use your lists to write sentences.**

1. Write a **telling sentence** about three cats.

_____

_____

2. Write an **asking sentence** about three cities.

_____

_____

42

3. Write an **exciting sentence** about three foods.

_____

_____

C **Write contractions for the words below.**

1. did not _____ *didn't* _____   **6.** cannot _____ *can't* _____

2. you are _____ *you're* _____   **7.** we have _____ *we've* _____

3. I am _____ *I'm* _____   **8.** has not _____ *hasn't* _____

4. it is _____ *it's* _____   **9.** is not _____ *isn't* _____

5. they will _____ *they'll* _____   **10.** she is _____ *she's* _____

D **Fill in each blank with a word that shows ownership.**

1. The dog has a ball. It is the _____ *dog's* _____ ball.

2. Alisha has a computer. It is _____ *Alisha's* _____ computer.

3. Our teacher has a bike. It is our _____ *teacher's* _____ bike.

4. Barry has a pet bird. It is _____ *Barry's* _____ pet bird.

Name
_____

Capital Letters for Names and Titles

Use **capital letters** for people's names and titles.

title   **name**

↘   ↙

Mr. Thomas lives in a little house.
Mrs. Thomas lives there, too.

A Add capital letters where they are needed. Cross out the lower-case letter you want to change. Write the correct capital letter above it.

                           M C

1. Our class helper is mrs. cantu.

                         M T

2. The school nurse is mr. thomas.

            W   D P

3. Yesterday, will and I went to see dr. paula.

         M D

4. I asked ms. demarko to read me a story.

         M C

5. Mr. and mrs. chang picked us up at camp.

         M B   S

6. Tomorrow, ms. banks and sally are coming over.

         D V

7. Our dentist is dr. villa.

B Draw a picture or paste a photo of your favorite grown-up.

Write two sentences telling why you like this grown-up. Make sure to use the grown-up's title and name each time.

1. _____

_____

2. _____

_____

Name

Capital Letters for Days of the Week 1

Use **capital letters** for days of the week.

Sunday **W**ednesday

Monday
December
14

A Answer the questions below. Remember to use capital letters correctly.

1. Which day comes after Saturday? _____Sunday_____

2. Which day is between Tuesday and Thursday?

_____Wednesday_____

3. Which day begins with the letter "F"? _____Friday_____

4. Which day is the first day of the school week?

_____Monday_____

5. Which day comes after Friday? _____Saturday_____

6. Which day is before Wednesday? _____Tuesday_____

7. Which day comes before Friday? _____Thursday_____

46

 B **Put the days of the week in the correct order, starting with Sunday.**

Thursday   Sunday   Tuesday   Monday

Friday   Wednesday   Saturday

1. _____Sunday_____   5. _____Thursday_____

2. _____Monday_____   6. _____Friday_____

3. _____Tuesday_____   7. _____Saturday_____

4. _____Wednesday_____

Write a sentence about your favorite day of the week.

_____

_____

_____

Name _____

Capital Letters for Days of the Week 2

Use **capital letters** for days of the week.

↗Saturday
↗Thursday

A   Write each day of the week with a capital letter.

1. Mr. Shaw will be here tuesday, March 13.

Tuesday
_____

2. The party was on friday, September 23.

Friday
_____

3. School starts monday, August 16.

Monday
_____

4. Kathleen's birthday is wednesday, April 29.

Wednesday
_____

5. Valentine's Day will be thursday, February 14.

Thursday
_____

B Put a capital letter at the beginning of each day of the week.

Everyone in my family was born on a different

day of the week. Mom was born on a ~~t~~uesday, but
                                        T

dad was born on a ~~f~~riday. My sister Lisa was born
                    F

on a ~~t~~hursday night, and I was born early one
       T

~~s~~aturday morning. Then my brand new dog Biscuit
S

was born last ~~s~~unday!
               S

Write two sentences about activities you have on certain days.

1. _____

   _____

2. _____

   _____

Name _____

Capital Letters for Months of the Year 1

Use **capital letters** for the months of the year.

February   May

A **Use capital letters for the months in these sentences.**

               M

1. The first day of spring is in march.

           J

2. The first day of summer is in june.

        S

3. The first day of fall is in september.

        D

4. The first day of winter is in december.

        J

5. The first month of the year is january.

       F

6. The shortest month is february.

    J   A

7. Usually july and august are the hottest months.

 A

8. april showers bring spring flowers.

50

B Here are three more months. Write each month correctly.

may   _May_

october   _October_

november   _November_

Write one sentence about each month above.

1. _____

_____

_____

2. _____

_____

_____

3. _____

_____

_____

Name _____

Capital Letters for Months of the Year 2

Use **capital letters** for the months of the year.

 A   Read the sentences below. Write the month correctly on the line after each sentence.

1. Handwriting Day is the 12th of january. __January__

2. Groundhog Day is in february. __February__

3. Arbor Day is in april. __April__

4. Memorial Day is the last Monday in may. __May__

5. My birthday is in june. __June__

6. Independence Day is the fourth of july. __July__

7. Labor Day is in september. __September__

8. Fire Prevention Week is during october. __October__

9. Thanksgiving Day is in november. __November__

52

B Unscramble these months and write them correctly on the lines below. Remember to use a capital letter for the first letter!

1. uejn — June

2. gsatuu — August

3. hamrc — March

4. yrjnuaa — January

5. larip — April

6. yma — May

7. tbreoco — October

8. eeedmbcr — December

9. eyfbarru — February

10. ljuy — July

11. ervbnome — November

12. tpbreesme — September

Name _____

Capital Letters for Holidays

Use **capital letters** for the names of holidays.

↙   ↙
Father's Day   Thanksgiving Day

  A Use capital letters for the holidays in these sentences. (*Day* is part of many holiday names.)

     N   Y   D
1. new year's day is in January.

                             V   D
2. We made cards for valentine's day.

                      P   D
3. We celebrate presidents' day in February.

     M   D   M   D
4. mother's day and memorial day are always in May.

                               F   D
5. One holiday in June is flag day.

                  I   D
6. July 4 is independence day.

                                       L   D
7. The first Monday in September is labor day.

                                  C   D
8. The second Monday in October is columbus day.

54

B Write the names of three holidays found in the sentences on page 51.

1. _____

2. _____

3. _____

KEEP GOING

Now use the names of those three holidays in sentences.

1. _____

_____

_____

2. _____

_____

_____

3. _____

_____

_____

55

Name _____

Capital Letters
for Names of Places

Use a **capital letter** for the name
of a city, a state, or a country.

City	State	Country
Carson City	Nevada	France
Rome	Iowa	Mexico

 A **Write the city, state, or country correctly in the following sentences.**

1. *Make Way for Ducklings* takes place in the city of

   boston. _____ **Boston** _____

2. The Everglades are in florida. _____ Florida _____

3. My grandma is from ireland. _____ Ireland _____

4. Mt. Fuji is in japan. _____ Japan _____

5. The Willis Tower is in chicago. _____ Chicago _____

6. The Peach State is georgia. _____ Georgia _____

7. The capital of Alaska is juneau. _____ Juneau _____

B Write the answers to the following questions. Use correct capitalization.

1. Which city or town do you live in?

_____

2. Which state do you live in?

_____

3. What is one state that is near your home state?

_____

4. What city does the President of the United States live in?

_____

5. What country were you born in?

_____

6. Which country would you most like to visit?

_____

Name _____

Capital Letter for *I*

Use a **capital letter** for the word *I*.

↗I have curly red hair.

Cory and I like to tap-dance.

A Write the word *I* in each of these sentences.

1. Jimmy and ___I___ are friends.

2. Sometimes ___I___ go to his house.

3. ___I___ ride there on my bike.

4. Sometimes Jimmy and ___I___ play at the park.

B Write two sentences of your own using the word *I*.

1. _____

_____

2. _____

_____

58

Draw a picture of yourself in the box below. Then write three sentences about yourself. Use the word *I* in each sentence.

1. _____

_____

2. _____

_____

3. _____

_____

Name _____

Capital Letters to Begin Sentences

Always use a **capital letter** for the first word in a sentence.

We go to the park in the summer.

A Begin each of the following sentences with a capital letter.

1. O͟ne day we had a picnic.

2. A͟unt Jill brought a big bowl of fruit salad.

3. G͟randma made lemonade and biscuits.

4. W͟e had sub sandwiches and carrot sticks.

5. A͟ll the kids played softball before lunch.

6. A͟fter the game everyone drank lemonade.

7. G͟randma's biscuits were the best part of the picnic.

8. T͟he ants liked the crumbs we dropped.

60

Put a capital letter at the beginning of each sentence. Put a period at the end of each sentence.

T   S
there's a swimming pool at our park. sometimes

                      I
we go there for a swim. i learned how to swim last

N   M
year. now I can go in the deep end of the pool. my

                              S
little sister can't swim yet. she stays in the shallow

M
end. maybe I'll teach her how to swim.

Write two sentences about things you like to do in the summer. Remember to use capital letters and periods.

1. _____

_____

2. _____

_____

3. _____

_____

Name _____

Capital Letter for a Speaker's First Word

Use a **capital letter** for a speaker's
first word.

He asked, "**C**an you guess what this is?"

 Add capital letters where they are needed.

1. Our teacher asked, "<u>D</u>do you know the story of the blind

men and the elephant?"

2. "<u>I</u>i do," said Jasmine. "<u>O</u>one man feels the elephant's

trunk. <u>H</u>he thinks an elephant is like a big snake."

3. "<u>A</u>another man feels the ear," Kerry added. "<u>H</u>he thinks

an elephant is like a big fan."

4. Jasmine said, "<u>A</u>another man feels the leg. <u>H</u>he thinks an

elephant is like a tree trunk."

5. Then Ms. Tyler asked, "<u>H</u>how could they know the truth?"

6. Kerry said, "<u>T</u>they could work and talk together."

B Add capital letters where they are needed.

1. Ms. Tyler said, "$\overset{\text{T}}{\text{t}}$hat's right, Kerry."

2. She asked, "$\overset{\text{W}}{\text{w}}$hen do you like to work together?"

3. Kerry answered, "$\overset{\text{I}}{\text{i}}$ like working together to perform plays."

4. Jasmine added, "$\overset{\text{T}}{\text{t}}$hat's something one person can't usually do alone."

Complete this sentence telling what the elephant thinks about the blind men.

The elephant said, "_____

_____."

Name

Capital Letters for Book Titles

Most words in book titles begin with **capital letters.**

➤ <u>Town Mouse, Country Mouse</u>

Some words do not begin with capital letters (unless they are the first or last word of a title). Here are some examples:

a   an   the   and   but   of

to   with   by   for   on

 A   **Write the four underlined book titles correctly on the lines below.**

I went to the library yesterday. I found some wonderful books! I checked out <u>madison in new york</u>, <u>fishing with dad</u>, <u>hattie and the fox</u>, and <u>my brother needs a boa</u>.

1. <u>Madison in New York</u>

2. <u>Fishing with Dad</u>

3. <u>Hattie and the Fox</u>

4. <u>My Brother Needs a Boa</u>

B Write down the titles of your favorite book and magazine.

Book: _____

Magazine: _____

Write a note telling someone about your favorite book or magazine.

Dear _____ ,

_____

_____

_____

_____

_____

Your friend,

_____

Capital Letters for Greetings and Closings in Letters

Use a **capital letter** to begin the greeting and the closing in a letter.

Dear Grandpa,   **greeting or salutation**

    Thank you for the new jacket. It's my favorite color! You always know just what I like.

                 Love,
                 Sara **closing**

A Use capital letters to begin the greeting and closing in these letters.

July 1, 2010

dear Jake,

    Happy birthday!
I wish I could go
to your party. Will
you have a piñata?
       love,
       Erin

May 21, 2011

dear Mr. Murphy,

    Your dog Sonny
is one of the best
dogs. May I walk him
after school? I even
have my own leash.
       thank you,
       Justin

66

B Use capital letters to begin the greeting and closing in Aunt Molly's letter. Then pretend you are Harrison. Write what you would say back. Be sure to use capital letters in the right places.

D   July 14, 2010
dear Harrison,

   I hope you can come to Texas sometime soon. You have got to see the San Antonio River Walk! It's a great place to visit!

                              L
                              love,
                              Aunt Molly

_____
(Date)

_____
(Greeting or Salutation)

_____

_____

_____
(Closing)

_____
(Signature)

© Houghton Mifflin Harcourt Publishing Company

Name _____

Capital Letters Review

This activity reviews some of the different ways to use **capital letters**.

> **A** Put capital letters where they are needed. (There are 21 in all.) Watch for these things:
> * greetings and closings,
> * first word in a sentence,
> * names and titles of people, and
> * names of cities, states, and countries.

May 24, 2010

D   L
dear linny,

    O   M B
    our class is studying rivers. mr. banks read a
                        N   R   T
book to us about the nashua river. the book was
             L   C   W
written by lynne cherry. we also learned about the
N R   A   M J   S
nile river in africa. ms. johnson visited our class. she
                    A   R
went down the amazon river on a raft!
                                 L
                                love,
                               J
                               jim

Put capital letters where they are needed. (There are 11 in all.) Watch for:
 * **a speaker's first word.**
 * **names of days and months.**
 * **names of holidays.**

1. Joel said, "<u>M</u>my favorite day is <u>S</u>sunday. What's

yours?"

2. "<u>S</u>sunday is my favorite day, too," I answered.

3. "<u>W</u>what's your favorite month?" Molly asked.

4. I said, "<u>M</u>my favorite month is <u>J</u>july, because it's

summer, and that's when I was born."

5. Molly said, "<u>M</u>my favorite month is <u>D</u>december,

because that's when we celebrate <u>H</u>hanukkah."

6. "<u>T</u>that's when we celebrate <u>C</u>christmas," I said.

 Put capital letters where they are needed in these titles.

1. <u>T</u>the <u>T</u>tigger <u>M</u>movie   **2.** <u>T</u>the <u>F</u>fox and the <u>H</u>hound

Name _____

Plurals

Plural means more than one. For most nouns, make the plurals by adding **-s**.

desk → desk**s** window → window**s**

 A Here is a list of things that may be in your classroom. Write the plural forms of the nouns. Then tell a partner a sentence using the plural form of something else found in your classroom.

1. flag _____ flags

2. table _____ tables

3. eraser _____ erasers

4. pencil _____ pencils

5. book _____ books

6. marker _____ markers

7. door _____ doors

8. ruler _____ rulers

B Fill in the blanks by changing the singular word under the line into a plural word.

There are 16 ___girls___ and 10 ___boys___
         (girl)   *(boy)*

in my class this year. We have one teacher and two

___helpers___ . There are three learning
(helper)

___centers___ in the classroom. In the reading center
(center)

there are lots of ___magazines___ . The art center has
         (magazine)

some very bright ___markers___ . In the writing center
         (marker)

there's a whole box of ___pencils___ and many different
         (pencil)

___kinds___ of paper. I love my classroom!
(kind)

Write a sentence telling how many boys and girls there are in your class. Then tell a partner how many students are in your class using a complete sentence.

_____

_____

Name _____

Plurals Using -s and -es 1

For most nouns, make the **plurals** by adding **-s**.

one bird   two bird**s**
a bike   four bike**s**

For some nouns, you need to do more.
Add **-es** to words that end in **sh, ch, s,** or **x**.

a bush   some bush**es**
one box   two box**es**

A   Write the plurals of the following nouns. It's easy—just add **-s**. Then tell a sentence to a partner using one of the plural nouns.

1. bug   bugs   6. dog   dogs

2. river   rivers   7. house   houses

3. eye   eyes   8. desk   desks

4. ear   ears   9. tree   trees

5. sister   sisters   10. lake   lakes

72

B Make the following nouns plural. They all end in *sh*, *ch*, *s*, or *x*. You will need to add *-es*.

1. brush __brushes__   5. fax __faxes__
2. class __classes__   6. patch __patches__
3. bench __benches__   7. boss __bosses__

C Fill in each blank with the correct plural. You will need to add *-s* to some nouns and *-es* to other nouns. Then use one of the plural nouns in your own sentence and tell it to a partner.

1. At the petting zoo there are baby __lions__
   (lion)

   and __foxes__ .
   (fox)

2. There are three __hamsters__ and
   (hamster)

   two __gerbils__ in my classroom.
   (gerbil)

3. My mom makes __lunches__ for me and
   (lunch)

   my two __brothers__ .
   (brother)

© Houghton Mifflin Harcourt Publishing Company

Name _____

Plurals Using -s and -es 2

Make the **plurals** of most nouns by adding **-s**.

one snack   two snack**s**

For nouns that end in **sh**, **ch**, **s**, or **x**, add **-es** to make the plurals.

one lunch   two lunch**es**

A   Write the plurals of the following nouns. Add **-s** or **-es**.

1. apple   _apples_

2. carrot   _carrots_

3. dish   _dishes_

4. glass   _glasses_

5. spoon   _spoons_

6. box   _boxes_

7. peach   _peaches_

8. sandwich _sandwiches_

9. raisin   _raisins_

10. fork   _forks_

KEEP GOING

Draw a lunchbox on your own paper. Include some of the things you just listed. Tell a partner about your lunch.

74

Name _____

Words That Change to Make Plurals

A few nouns make their **plurals** by changing letters and words. Here are some examples of irregular plurals.

child – **children**   mouse – **mice**
foot – **feet**   wife – **wives**
goose – **geese**   woman – **women**
man – **men**   wolf – **wolves**

A **Fill in each blank with the correct plural from the nouns above. Then use one of the plural nouns to tell a partner a sentence of your own.**

1. There's a song about three blind _____*mice*_____.

2. You clap with your hands and walk with your ____*feet*____.

3. Ducks and _____*geese*_____ like to swim in ponds.

4. Sheep need to be protected from _____*wolves*_____.

5. Cartoons are for _____*children*_____, but____*men*____

and _____*women*_____ watch them, too.

6. Husbands have _____*wives*_____.

Name _____

Plurals of Words That End in *y* 1

Here are two rules for making **plurals** of nouns ending in *y*.

Rule 1   If there is a consonant right before the *y*, change the *y* to *i* and add *-es*.

one baby   two babies

Rule 2   If there is a vowel right before the *y*, just add *-s*.

one turkey → three turkeys

A   Write the plurals of the following nouns. Use rule 1. Then tell a partner a sentence using one of the plural nouns.

1. cherry   cherries   6. bunny   bunnies

2. kitty   kitties   7. pony   ponies

3. party   parties   8. puppy   puppies

4. berry   berries   9. country   countries

5. guppy   guppies   10. worry   worries

B Make the following nouns plural. Use rule 2 from page 75. Tell a partner a sentence using one of the plural nouns.

1. monkey ___monkeys___   **3.** toy ___toys___

2. ray ___rays___   **4.** holiday ___holidays___

KEEP GOING

Circle three of the plurals you made on pages 75–76. Use each one in a sentence.

1. _____

_____

2. _____

_____

3. _____

_____

Name _____

Plurals of Words That End in *y* 2

Here are two rules for making **plurals** of nouns ending in *y*.

Rule 1 If there is a consonant right before the *y*, change the *y* to *i* and add *-es*.

one ba**b**y   two bab**ies**

Rule 2 If there is a vowel right before the *y*, just add *-s*.

one turk**e**y   three turkey**s**

A Make the following nouns plural using rule 1 or rule 2. Then tell a partner a sentence using one of the plural nouns.

1. story _____ **stories** _____

2. diary _____ **diaries** _____

3. donkey _____ **donkeys** _____

4. key _____ **keys** _____

5. baby _____ **babies** _____

6. day _____ **days** _____

78

Name _____

Plurals Review

This activity reviews making **plurals**. After each set, practice speaking using plural nouns with a partner.

A Make these nouns plural by adding *-s* or *-es*.

1. glass _____glasses_____   4. bus _____buses_____

2. brush _____brushes_____   5. dress _____dresses_____

3. frog _____frogs_____   6. worm _____worms_____

B Make these nouns plural by adding *-s* or changing *y* to *i* and adding *-es*.

1. monkey _____monkeys_____   4. turkey _____turkeys_____

2. puppy _____puppies_____   5. toy _____toys_____

3. day _____days_____   6. cherry _____cherries_____

C Change these words to make them plural.

1. mouse _____mice_____   3. woman _____women_____

2. foot _____feet_____   4. knife _____knives_____

Name _____

Abbreviations

Put a **period** after a person's title.
Mr.   Mrs.   Ms.   Dr.

Ms. Walters   Mr. Johnson

A   **Put periods after the people's titles in these sentences.**

1. Mr. Forest is our next-door neighbor.

2. Mr. and Mrs. Forest have a very big garden.

3. Mrs. Forest works in her garden on cool mornings.

4. Her friend Dr. Maynard stops to visit before work.

5. Mrs. Forest gives Dr. Maynard some pretty flowers
to take to the office.

6. After dinner, Mr. Forest likes to weed the garden.

7. Mrs. Forest helps him water the plants.

B Think of four people who work in your school. Write their names below. Be sure to write Mr., Mrs., Ms., or Dr. before each.

1. _____

2. _____

3. _____

4. _____

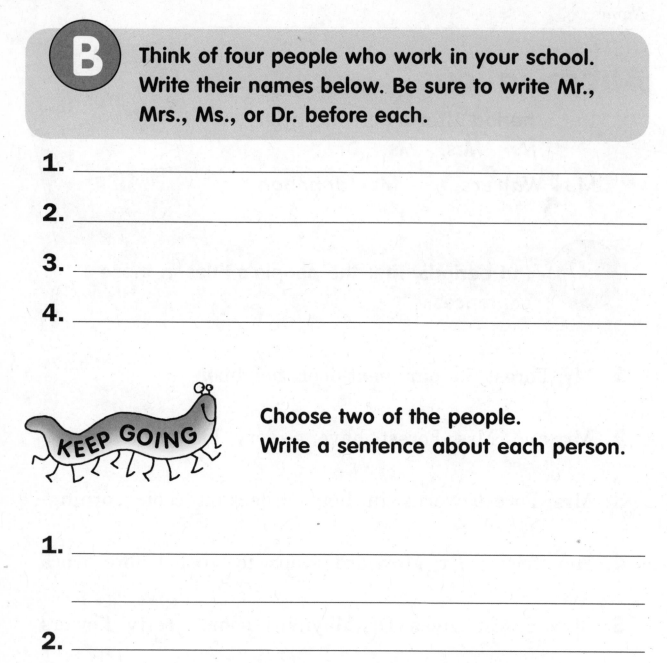

KEEP GOING

Choose two of the people.
Write a sentence about each person.

1. _____

_____

2. _____

_____

Name _____

Abbreviations for Days and Months

When writing sentences, you should write the full names of the days and the months.

Today is **Tuesday, October 9.**

You should also know the **abbreviations** for the names of the days and the months.

Tuesday ➜ Tues.   October ➜ Oct.

 A Write the abbreviations for the days and months in the following lists.

1. Sunday ___Sun.___   **7.** February ___Feb.___

2. Friday ___Fri.___   **8.** March ___Mar.___

3. Wednesday ___Wed.___   **9.** November ___Nov.___

4. Thursday ___Thurs.___   **10.** August ___Aug.___

5. Saturday ___Sat.___   **11.** September ___Sept.___

6. Monday ___Mon.___   **12.** January ___Jan.___

82

Name

Post Office Abbreviations

The US Postal Service suggests using all capital letters and no periods in abbreviations.

948 **N** LINCOLN
North

A Read the addresses below. Write the words for the underlined abbreviations.

1. 1060 W ADDISON <u>ST</u>

Street

2. 1600 PENNSYLVANIA <u>AVE</u>

Avenue

3. 28 <u>E</u> 20TH ST

East

4. 7400 GRANT <u>RD</u>

Road

5. 413 <u>S</u> EIGHTH STREET

South

6. 40 PRESIDENTIAL <u>DR</u>

Drive

Name _____

Checking Mechanics Review 1

This activity reviews some of the ways to use capital letters.

 A **Put capital letters where they are needed. There are 21 for you to find.**

D T
dear theresa,

    H   H   F   T   M
    how are you? how is life in florida? today ms.
M   I
martinez said she wished we could all visit you. i

           I   J
told her i get to visit you in june!

   I   L P P I
    i just read a book called lon po po. it is a

good story from china. lee gave me the book for my

birthday.

   M   J
    mrs. james said she hopes you like your new

            D
school. do you?

                         Your friend,

                         Roger

84

B Fill in the blanks below. Use your *Write Source* if you need help.

1. Write two days of the week that are school days:

   _____   _____

2. Write the name of a holiday: _____

3. Write your first name: _____

4. Write the name of a planet: _____

5. Write your teacher's name: _____

Now use the words you just wrote to complete this story.

It was _____ , but there was no school. It
      (day of the week)

was _____ . _____ had a busy
    (name of the holiday)   *(teacher's name)*

day planned. _____ was going to build a
             (your name)

spaceship and blast off to _____ .
                           (planet)

Name _____

Checking Mechanics Review 2

This activity reviews plurals and abbreviations.

 Write the plural of each animal name.

1. cow   <u>cows</u>
2. donkey   <u>donkeys</u>
3. finch   <u>finches</u>
4. goose   <u>geese</u>
5. guppy   <u>guppies</u>

6. mouse   <u>mice</u>
7. fox   <u>foxes</u>
8. pig   <u>pigs</u>
9. puppy   <u>puppies</u>
10. turkey   <u>turkeys</u>

 Write the abbreviation for each day of the week.

1. Monday   <u>Mon.</u>
2. Tuesday   <u>Tues.</u>
3. Wednesday   <u>Wed.</u>
4. Thursday   <u>Thurs.</u>

5. Friday   <u>Fri.</u>
6. Saturday   <u>Sat.</u>
7. Sunday   <u>Sun.</u>

C Write the abbreviations for the months of the year. Notice some months are not abbreviated.

1. January   Jan.

2. February   Feb.

3. March   Mar.

4. April   Apr.

5. May   May

6. June   June

7. July   July

8. August   Aug.

9. September   Sept.

10. October   Oct.

11. November   Nov.

12. December   Dec.

Name _____

Using the Right Word 1

Some words sound alike, but they have different spellings. They also have different meanings. These words are **homophones**. Here are two examples:

My **bare** hands are cold.

I saw a **bear** at the zoo.

A   **Fill in each blank with** *bare* **or** *bear*.

1. The panda ____bear____ lives in China.

2. Our teacher puts a rug on the ____bare____ floor.

3. This morning I found a picture of a koala ____bear____ .

4. Bees stung the boy's ____bare____ legs.

5. The sun felt warm on my ____bare____ arms.

B   **Write a sentence using** *bare* **and** *bear*.

_____

_____

88

C Fill in each blank with *ate* or *eight* or *ant* or *aunt*.

Suzzie **ate** two carrots today.
Spiders have **eight** legs.

I watched an **ant** crawl up the wall.
My **aunt** lives across town.

1. Last year my _____aunt_____ visited friends in California.

2. A carpenter _____ant_____ loves to eat wood.

3. I counted _____eight_____ sparrows sitting on the ground.

4. An _____ant_____ can walk on the ceiling.

5. I can pick up _____eight_____ rocks with one hand.

6. For lunch, I _____ate_____ a cheese sandwich.

7. Sarai's _____aunt_____ _____ate_____ a tasty apple.

D Write a sentence using *ate* and *eight*.

_____

_____

Name _____

Using the Right Word 2

Some words sound alike, but they have different spellings. They also have different meanings. These words are **homophones**. Here are two examples:

The **deer** eat acorns.   My aunt is **dear** to me.

 A **Fill in each blank with *blew* or *blue*.**

The wind **blew** all day.
Some houses are painted **blue**.

1. Is _____**blue**_____ the color of the sky?

2. Please pick up a _____**blue**_____ worksheet today.

3. That girl just _____**blew**_____ a huge bubble.

4. Will you put this book on the _____**blue**_____ shelf?

5. The sign just _____**blew**_____ over.

 B **Write a sentence using *dear* and *deer*.**

_____

_____

C Fill in each blank with *by* or *buy*.

Your pencil is **by** the dictionary.
I want to **buy** a notebook.

1. Can you ____buy____ a bicycle for ten cents?

2. My best friend is waiting ____by____ the oak

tree in the park.

3. Will wants to ____buy____ a birthday present

for Samuel.

4. The book ____by____ the teacher's desk

belongs to Maria.

5. Go stand ____by____ the school bus.

D Write a sentence using *for* and *four*.

_____

_____

Name _____

Using the Right Word 3

Some words sound alike, but they have different spellings. They also have different meanings. These words are **homophones**. Here are some examples:

I **hear** you.   I *am* **here**.

 A Fill in each blank with *here* or *hear*.

1. I asked my dog Dan to come _____here_____ .

2. Can you _____hear_____ what I am saying?

3. Did you _____hear_____ what happened to Sara?

4. _____Here_____ is the ball I thought I lost.

B Fill in each blank with *no* or *know*.

Anna said, **"No,** I didn't **know** that."

1. There is _____no_____ more soup.

2. I _____know_____ where to get some.

3. Just answer yes or _____no_____ .

4. Do you _____know_____ the new girl?

C Fill in each blank with *new* or *knew*.

These shoes are **new**.   I **knew** the answer.

1. I got a _____ **new** _____ raincoat.

2. My mom _____ **knew** _____ it was going to rain today.

3. Mike said he _____ **knew** _____ how it would end.

4. My sister got _____ **new** _____ boots.

D Fill in each blank with *its* or *it's*.

It's washing **its** kitten.

1. The cat uses _____ **its** _____ tongue.

2. _____ **It's** _____ washing the kitten's fur.

3. The kitten needs _____ **its** _____ mother.

4. _____ **It's** _____ fun to watch the kitten grow.

E Write a sentence using *its* and *it's*.

_____

_____

Name _____

Using the Right Word 4

Some words sound alike, but they have different spellings. They also have different meanings. These words are **homophones**. Here are some examples:

I have **two** cats.
I have a dog, **too**.
I go **to** Pine Elementary.

 A   **Fill in each blank with** *two*, *to*, **or** *too*. *Too* **can mean "also" or "more than enough."**

1. We are going _____**to**_____ the beach.

2. We can only stay for _____**two**_____ hours.

3. Can Marla come, _____**too**_____ ?

4. I like to take a radio _____**to**_____ the beach.

5. Just don't play it _____**too**_____ loud.

 B   **Write a sentence using** *two* **and** *to*.

_____

_____

C Fill in each blank with *one* or *won*.

One summer I **won** a ribbon.

1. There was _____one_____ race.

2. I was so fast, I _____won_____.

3. Mr. Wang gave me _____one_____ blue ribbon.

4. I showed it to _____one_____ of my cousins.

5. My mom couldn't believe I _____won_____.

D Fill in each blank with *their*, *there*, or *they're*.

We saw **their** new puppy. (*Their* shows ownership.)

There are three pets now.

They're lots of fun. (*They're* = they are.)

1. _____There_____ are four kids in the Clark family.

2. We play freeze tag in _____their_____ backyard.

3. _____They're_____ my next-door neighbors.

4. I went to school _____there_____ for one year.

Name _____

Using the Right Word
Review 1

This activity reviews the
homophones you have practiced.

 A Write the correct word in each blank.

1. Sam took _____two_____ rats _____to_____ school.
    (two, to, too)   *(two, to, too)*

2. The white rat _____ate_____ all of _____its_____ food.
    (eight, ate)   *(its, it's)*

3. Someone yelled, "Don't bring them in _____here_____!"
                    (hear, here)

4. "I don't like _____their_____ _____bare_____ tails!"
    (they're, their, there)   *(bear, bare)*

5. Miss Green said, "I _____know_____ what to do."
              (no, know)

6. "We'll get a box _____for_____ the rats to sleep in."
              (for, four)

7. Other students have pets _____too_____ .
              (two, to, too)

8. Don has a ___new___ pet parrot.
(new, knew)

9. ___There___ are more than 300 kinds of parrots.
(Their, There, They're)

10. Don will ___buy___ a book about parrots.
(buy, by)

11. Then he will ___know___ how to care for his pet.
(no, know)

12. You should ___hear___ the parrot talk!
(hear, here)

B Write three sentences. Use one of these words in each sentence: *to*, *two*, *too*.

1. _____

_____

2. _____

_____

3. _____

_____

Name _____

Using the Right Word Review 2

 Before each sentence is a group of words. Choose the correct word to fill in each blank.

1. **(hear, here)** "Did you ___hear___ that Uncle Andy and

   Aunt Sue are coming ___here___ ?" I asked.

2. **(know, no)** "Well, ___no___ , I didn't ___know___

   that," Lea answered.

3. **(Ant, Aunt)** ___Aunt___ Sue got a sailboat," I said. "She

   painted a red ___ant___ on the side of the boat."

4. **(their, there, they're)** "I hope ___they're___ bringing

   ___their___ boat when they come," Lea said.

5. **(knew, new)** "Sure," I said. "They ___knew___ we'd

   want to sail in the ___new___ boat."

98

B Below are three homophone pairs. Pick one pair, and draw a picture showing those words. (Use *Write Source* if you need to check meanings.) Then write a sentence about your picture.

one won   blew blue   dear deer

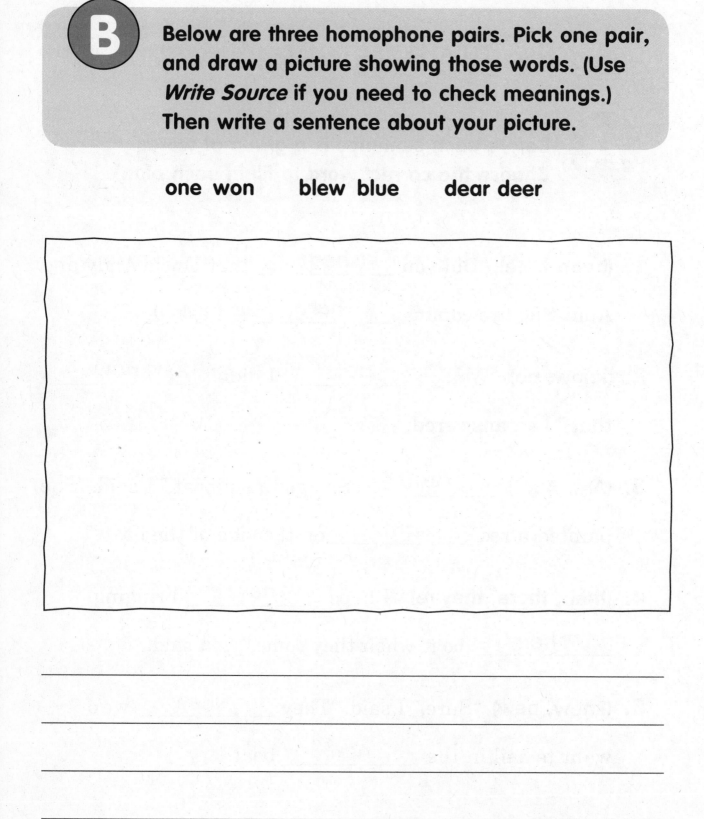

_____

_____

_____

_____

© Houghton Mifflin Harcourt Publishing Company

Sentence Activities

This section includes activities related to basic sentence writing, kinds of sentences, and sentence problems. In addition, **KEEP GOING**, which is at the end of many activities, encourages follow-up practice of certain skills.

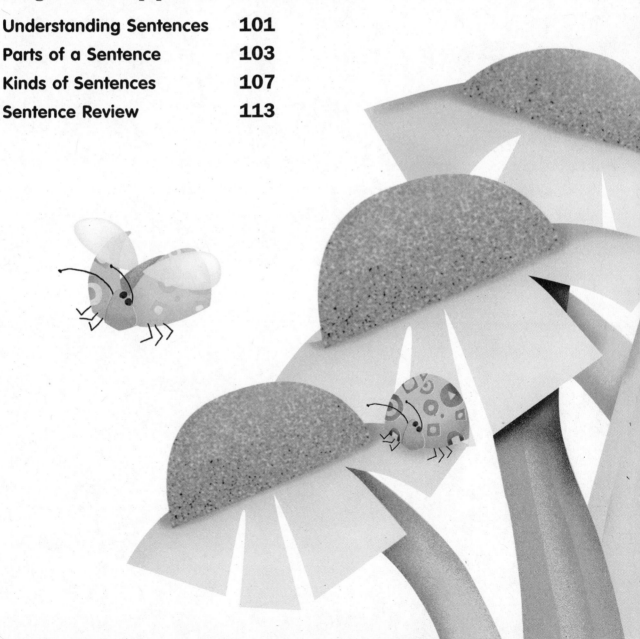

Name _____

Understanding Sentences

A **sentence** tells a complete thought.

This is not a complete thought:
On the window.

This is a complete thought:
A bug is on the window.

A Check whether each group of words is a complete thought or not.

	Complete Thought	
	Yes	**No**
1. From the downstairs music room.		✓
2. The sound was very loud.	✓	
3. Covered his ears.		✓
4. After that.		✓
5. He shut the front door.	✓	
6. Max played the drums.	✓	
7. Ming played the piano.	✓	
8. Mom the silver flute.		✓

B Fill in each blank with a word that completes the thought.

1. _____ was playing with a ball.

2. The _____ rolled down the hill.

3. _____ ran after it.

4. Then a big, hairy _____ ran after it, too.

5. The _____ got the ball and kept running.

6. Was the _____ gone for good?

Draw a picture about sentence 4.

Name _____

Parts of a Sentence 1

Every **sentence** has two parts, the **subject** and the **predicate**. The subject is the naming part. The predicate tells what the subject is doing. It always includes the verb.

Joe planted a seed.

subject ↗   ↖ predicate

The dirt covered the seed.

subject ↗   ↖ predicate

A Underline the subject with one line. Underline the predicate with two lines.

1. Joe watered his seed every day.

2. He watched it carefully.

3. A leaf popped out.

4. The leaf grew larger.

5. A flower bloomed one morning.

6. Joe told his mom.

Write a verb for each sentence.

1. Mom _____ bread.

2. I _____ her.

3. I _____ the flour.

4. I _____ the bowls.

5. Mom _____ the bread in the oven.

6. I always _____ the first slice of bread.

C **Check whether the underlined words are the subject or the predicate of the sentence.**

	Subject	Predicate
1. Your body <u>has a lot of bones</u>.		✓
2. <u>Your longest bone</u> is in your leg.	✓	
3. Your ribs <u>look like a cage</u>.		✓
4. Your smallest bone <u>is in your ear</u>.		✓
5. <u>Jellyfish</u> have no bones.	✓	
6. <u>A skeleton</u> is all bones.	✓	

Name _____

Parts of a Sentence 2

Every **sentence** has two parts, the **subject**
and the **predicate**. The subject is the naming part.
The predicate tells what the subject is doing. It
always includes the verb.

<u>Haley</u> <u>came to the party.</u>

subject ↗   ↖predicate

A Fill in each blank with a word from the box. You
may use some words more than once. These
words are the subjects in your sentences.

Poems	Ms. Day	Sam	Tacos
Eddy	Winter	Roses	Sarah

(Answers will vary.)

1. _____ plays on the soccer team.

2. Last summer, _____ drove to Ohio.

3. _____ grow in Grandpa's garden.

4. _____ are my favorite food.

5. _____ sleeps in a tent.

B Fill in each blank with a verb from the box. You will use each word only once. Each verb will be included in the predicate part of the sentence.

learned	barked	is	went
hit	sang	eats	gave

1. Bobby _____hit_____ a home run.

2. The dog _____barked_____ loudly.

3. Steve _____eats_____ toast every morning.

4. Our teacher _____gave_____ us a test.

5. Kerry _____sang_____ a song for the class.

6. At camp, Cheri _____learned_____ to ride a horse.

7. My sister's name _____is_____ Gail.

8. We all _____went_____ for a hike yesterday.

Name _____

Kinds of Sentences 1

A **telling sentence** makes a statement.
Put a period after a telling sentence.

Buster is out in the rain.

An **asking sentence** asks a question. Put
a question mark after an asking sentence.

Where is Buster?

 **Write *T* before each telling sentence, and put
a period after it. Write *A* before each asking
sentence, and put a question mark after it. Then
ask a partner a question and have him or her
answer it with a telling sentence.**

__A__   **1.** What is Sandy doing?

__T__   **2.** Sandy is making a bird feeder.

__A__   **3.** Why is she doing that?

__T__   **4.** She wants to see what kinds of birds will come.

__A__   **5.** Where will she put the bird feeder?

__T__   **6.** She's going to hang it in a tree.

__A__   **7.** What kind of food will she put in it?

B Draw a picture of some birds at a bird feeder.

KEEP GOING

Write one telling sentence and one asking sentence about your picture. Then have a partner ask you a question about your picture. Answer with a telling sentence.

1. Telling Sentence:_____

_____

2. Asking Sentence:_____

_____

Name _____

Kinds of Sentences 2

A **telling sentence** makes a statement.
Put a period after a telling sentence.
I'll feed Buster.

An **asking sentence** asks a question. Put
a question mark after an asking sentence.
Would you feed Buster, please?

 A **Write a telling sentence that is an answer for each asking sentence. Make sure you write complete sentences. Then ask a partner which question they liked answering best.**

(Answers will vary.)

1. What happened to your shoes?

_____

2. Who left the door open?

_____

3. How did you get all muddy?

_____

4. Have you read Too Many Tamales?

_____

110

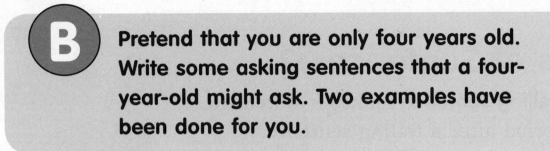

B Pretend that you are only four years old. Write some asking sentences that a four-year-old might ask. Two examples have been done for you.

1. _Where do bugs come from?_

2. _Why does it get dark at night?_

3. _____

4. _____

5. _____

Pick two questions from above. Write telling sentences to answer them. (Write interesting answers that are complete sentences!) Then pick another question and tell your answer to a partner.

1. _____

_____

2. _____

_____

© Houghton Mifflin Harcourt Publishing Company

Name _____

Subject-Verb Agreement in Sentences

Subjects and **verbs** must agree in number.

A **singular** subject must have a singular verb.

    I am at school today.

    ↗   ↖

Subject   Verb

A **plural** subject must have a plural verb.

    We are at school today.

    ↗   ↖

  Subject   Verb

 A   **Write the verb that goes with the subject of each sentence.**

1. Sometimes we _____**have**_____ a fire drill at school.

                  (has, have)

2. Mrs. Miller _____**is**_____ is our fire marshall.

                (is, are)

3. She _____**wears**_____ an orange vest so we can see her.

        (wear, wears)

4. We _____**walk**_____ in one straight line.

        (walk, walks)

5. Everyone _____**feels**_____ happy that it isn't a real fire!

        (feel, feels)

B Fill in each blank with *have* or *has*.

1. We _____ **have** _____ cousins living in the country.

2. Our cousins _____ **have** _____ a farm.

3. The farm _____ **has** _____ a house and barn.

4. The barn _____ **has** _____ cows and horses inside.

C Fill in each blank with *run* or *runs*.

1. All the horses _____ **run** _____ really fast.

2. Patty's horse _____ **runs** _____ in the front.

3. The other horses _____ **run** _____ behind her horse.

4. My horse _____ **runs** _____ on the side of the road!

D Describe your home to a partner using the verbs *is* and *are*. Use correct subject-verb agreement.

Name _____

Sentence Review

This reviews what you have learned about sentences.

 Write *S* after each sentence. Write *X* after each group of words that is not a sentence.

1. My dad and I. _____X_____

2. Went to Blue Hills Park. _____X_____

3. We hiked to the top of a big hill. _____S_____

4. Above the clouds! _____X_____

5. Then Treasure Cave. _____X_____

6. It was scary and dark inside. _____S_____

7. Later, we saw three fat raccoons. _____S_____

8. We had a lot of fun. _____S_____

9. Will visit the park again. _____X_____

 Read page 356 in your *Write Source* to see how the writer made one group of words a complete thought.

Underline and label the subjects and the predicates in the sentences that begin with *I*. The first sentence has been done for you.

May 26, 2011

Dear Grandma,

　　　　　　　　　　　S　　　　　P　　　　　S　　　　P
　　Guess what? <u>I</u> <u>lost another tooth!</u> <u>I</u> <u>bit into an apple.</u>

S　　　　　　　　P
<u>I</u> <u>feel the new hole in my mouth now.</u>

　　　　　　　　　　　　　　　　　　　　　　　　　　　　　S
　　Mom will bring me to your house next week. <u>I</u> <u>like</u>

P　　　　　S　　　　　　　　P
<u>your yard.</u> <u>I</u> <u>think your new slide is great!</u>

　　Will you make smoothies for me? See you soon.

　　　　　　　Love,

　　　　　　　John

Copy one telling sentence from the letter. Discuss with a partner if the sentence has correct subject-verb agreement.

1. Telling Sentence: _____

_____

Language Activities

The activities in this section are related to the parts of speech. All of the activities have a page link to *Write Source*. In addition, **KEEP GOING**, which is at the end of many activities, encourages follow-up practice of certain skills.

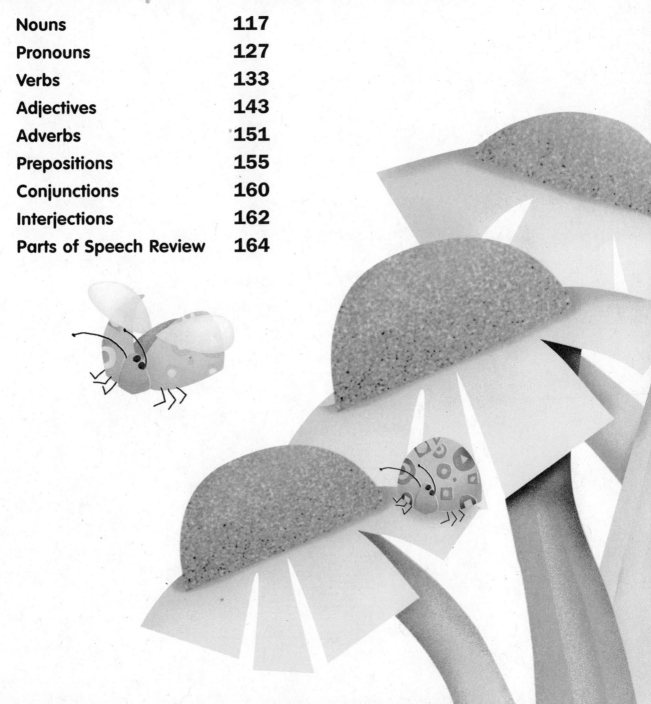

Name _____

Nouns

A **noun** names a person, a place, or a thing.

Person	Place	Thing
student	park	pizza
friend	mall	candle

 A   Write what each noun is: *person, place,* or *thing.*
Add three nouns of your own.

1. firefighter   <u>   person   </u>

2. library   <u>   place   </u>

3. hammer   <u>   thing   </u>

4. teacher   <u>   person   </u>

5. pencil   <u>   thing   </u>

6. store   <u>   place   </u>

7. _____

8. _____

9. _____

B Write **N** if the word is a noun. Write **X** if the word is not a noun.

N **1.** paper   X **4.** bring   X **7.** and

X **2.** go   N **5.** girl   X **8.** hot

N **3.** bee   N **6.** store   N **9.** kite

C Underline the noun in each sentence.

1. The <u>bus</u> is yellow.   **4.** Look at the <u>duck</u>!

2. The <u>spider</u> jumped.   **5.** The <u>sky</u> looks pretty.

3. This <u>game</u> is hard.   **6.** A <u>friend</u> called.

Write a sentence about your favorite toys. Then underline the nouns in your sentence.

_____

_____

_____

Name _____

Common and Proper Nouns 1

A **common noun** names a person, place, or thing.
A **proper noun** names a special person, place, or thing.

Common Noun	Proper Noun
boy	Tony Prada
school	Hill Elementary
city	Lexington

A proper noun begins with a capital letter.
Some proper nouns are more than one word.

A Underline the common noun in each sentence. Then tell a partner a sentence with a common noun and a proper noun. Have your partner identify each kind of noun.

1. The <u>class</u> is busy writing.

2. Our <u>teacher</u> likes to help.

3. A <u>girl</u> is reading quietly.

4. The <u>street</u> is shiny and wet.

5. This sandy <u>beach</u> is hot.

6. Let's swim in the <u>pool</u>!

B Underline the proper noun in each sentence.

1. We stopped at <u>Jefferson Library</u>.

2. <u>Susie</u> wanted a book about horses.

3. This book is about <u>President Lincoln</u>.

4. <u>Principal Brown</u> visited the library.

5. He speaks <u>Spanish</u>.

6. <u>Rosa Perez</u> does, too.

C Write *C* if the underlined word is a common noun. Write *P* if the underlined word is a proper noun. Then tell a partner your own sentences using common and proper nouns.

_C_ **1.** My neighbor walks her <u>dog</u> each afternoon.

_P_ **2.** My neighbor's name is <u>Mrs. Lee</u>.

_C_ **3.** Her dog likes <u>treats</u>.

_P_ **4.** <u>Alf</u> is a funny dog.

_C_ **5.** One day he got on a <u>bus</u>.

Name _____

Common and Proper Nouns 2

A **common noun** names any person, place, or thing. A **proper noun** names a special person, place, or thing.

Common Noun	Proper Noun
holiday	New Year's Day
country	Mexico

A proper noun begins with a capital letter. Some proper nouns are more than one word.

A Write *C* if the word is a common noun. Write *P* if the word is a proper noun. Choose two nouns from below to say in a sentence.

_C_ **1.** cat

_P_ **2.** Sun Park

_C_ **3.** library

_P_ **4.** Washington, D.C.

_C_ **5.** flag

_P_ **6.** Jennifer

_P_ **7.** Main Street

_C_ **8.** book

_C_ **9.** mountain

_P_ **10.** Rocky Mountains

B Draw a line from each common noun to the proper noun that fits with it.

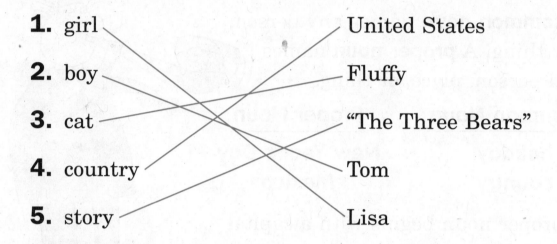

1. girl   United States

2. boy   Fluffy

3. cat   "The Three Bears"

4. country   Tom

5. story   Lisa

C Write *C* if the underlined noun is a common noun. Write *P* if the underlined noun is a proper noun. Choose your favorite noun from below. Use it in a sentence that you tell to a partner.

__P__ **1.** Today is <u>Christmas</u>!

__C__ **2.** There is no <u>school</u> today.

__C__ **3.** The <u>air</u> is freezing cold.

__P__ **4.** <u>Aunt Lizzie</u> visited us.

__C__ **5.** Kevin brought <u>popcorn</u>.

__P__ **6.** Chin is from <u>Korea</u>.

123

Name _____

Singular and Plural Nouns

Singular means one.

elephant

Plural means more than one.
elephants

Plural nouns usually end with **s**.

A Write *S* if the noun is singular. Write *P* if the noun is plural. Tell a partner a sentence using a plural noun and a singular noun from below.

__P__ **1.** boxes   __S__ **4.** rug

__S__ **2.** table   __S__ **5.** truck

__P__ **3.** chairs   __P__ **6.** toys

B Write *S* if the underlined noun is singular. Write *P* if the underlined noun is plural.

__S__ **1.** I like <u>art</u>.   __P__ **3.** <u>Paints</u> are messy.

__P__ **2.** I have <u>crayons</u>.   __S__ **4.** It's for my <u>sister</u>.

C **Underline the plural noun in each sentence.**

1. The cow has black and white <u>spots</u>.

2. Some <u>piglets</u> are pink.

3. <u>Potatoes</u> spilled out of the grocery bag.

4. My sister baked dinner <u>rolls</u> yesterday.

5. Tony took off his muddy <u>shoes</u>.

6. Erin held the tiny <u>kittens</u>.

Draw a picture about one of the plural nouns you underlined. Write the noun under your picture. Discuss your picture with a partner.

Name _____

Possessive Nouns

A **possessive noun** shows ownership.
A possessive noun has an **apostrophe**.

> **Tia's** toy boat was left out in the yard.
> (The toy boat belongs to Tia.)

> After the storm, we found it in the **dog's** house.
> (The house belongs to the dog.)

 A **Circle the possessive nouns.**

1. (Mike's) story about Mr. Bug was fun to read.

2. Mr. (Bug's) house was flooded when it rained.

3. Mr. (Bug's) family hopped in a toy boat.

4. All the little Bugs waited for the (storm's) end.

5. Finally, the boat floated to a (dog's) house.

6. The (dog's) name was Buddy.

7. The little Bugs asked if they could share their new (friend's) home.

8. The (story's) title is "The Bugs Find a Buddy."

B **Draw a picture of one of these things from the story:**

   * **Mr. Bug's flooded house**
   * **the child's toy boat**
   * **the dog's house**

Talk with a partner about your picture. Use a possessive noun.

Name _____

Pronouns 1

A **pronoun** is a word that takes the place of a noun.

Noun	Pronoun
Todd did it.	**He** did it.
Sally laughed.	**She** laughed.
The **rope** broke.	**It** broke.
The **skates** are too big.	**They** are too big.

 Circle the pronouns that replace the underlined nouns in the sentences below. Then say a sentence using each of the pronouns below.

1. <u>Holly</u> gave Katy a Mexican coin.

(She) gave Katy a Mexican coin.

2. Katy put the <u>coin</u> in a safe place.

Katy put (it) in a safe place.

3. <u>Peggy and Jo</u> wanted to see the coin.

(They) wanted to see the coin.

4. Then <u>Jay</u> asked to see it, too.

Then (he) asked to see it, too.

128

B Draw a line from each noun to the pronoun that could replace it. Then tell a partner a story using the nouns and pronouns below.

1. Dad and Mom   he
2. the girl   it
3. Grandpa   I
4. the TV   we
5. Shari and I   they
6. _____   she
(write your first name here)

C In each sentence, write a pronoun to replace the noun. If you need help, check the list of pronouns on page 334 in *Write Source*.

1. _____They_____ went to a movie.
   (Jim and Ray)

2. _____He_____ broke his arm.
   (The boy)

3. A doctor fixed _____it_____.
   (the arm)

4. _____She_____ is a good writer.
   (Jane)

Name _____

Pronouns 2

A **pronoun** can take the place of a possessive noun. A possessive noun shows ownership.

Noun	**Pronoun**
Jan's bicycle	her bicycle
Dave's skateboard	his skateboard
the bird's wing	its wing
Mike and Laura's poem	their poem

 A Circle the pronouns that take the place of the underlined nouns in the sentences below. Then say sentences using the pronouns below.

1. <u>Juanita's</u> coat is red.

(Her) coat is hanging up.

2. At the picnic, <u>Jake's</u> lunch fell into the water.

(His) lunch was soggy.

3. Yesterday <u>Sam and Sarah</u> missed the bus.

(Their) bus left early.

4. The <u>dog</u> was very excited.

(It) chewed on a big bone.

B Underline the pronoun in each sentence. Draw a picture of the pet rat. Then discuss pets you know with a partner using pronouns.

1. Here is <u>my</u> pet rat.

2. Dad likes <u>its</u> pink ears.

3. Mom likes <u>its</u> long tail.

4. Bogart is <u>our</u> favorite pet.

5. <u>He</u> has red eyes.

6. Ted pets <u>his</u> white fur.

7. <u>We</u> bought a blue cage.

C Draw a line to the pronoun that could replace the underlined words.

1. I heard <u>Tim and Judy's</u> song.   ours

2. I know <u>your sister's</u> name.   Its

3. Here comes <u>Ricky's</u> friend.   their

4. <u>The book's</u> cover got wet.   his

5. The tree house is <u>yours and mine</u>.   her

Name _____

Pronouns 3

A **pronoun** is a word that takes the place of a noun.

Jason *made a* **sandwich.**
Then **he** *ate* **it.**
(The pronouns *he* and *it* take the place of the nouns *Jason* and *sandwich.*)

 Fill in each blank with a pronoun that replaces the underlined word or words. Then say a few sentences using the pronouns *they* and *we*.

1. <u>Joe and Ann</u> read a poem. ___**They**___ read it aloud.

2. <u>Tanya</u> drew a map. ___**She**___ showed it to me.

3. <u>My brother and I</u> have a clubhouse. ___**We**___ made it ourselves.

4. I hope you're coming to my <u>party</u>. ___**It**___ will be fun.

5. Mom heard our <u>music</u>. ___**It**___ was too loud.

6. <u>Tony</u> is coming over. ___**He**___ is my friend.

7. The <u>monkeys</u> ate bananas. ___**They**___ were hungry.

8. This <u>book</u> is great. ___**It**___ has good pictures, too.

B Use each pronoun in a sentence.

| I | we | she | they |

1. _____

2. _____

3. _____

4. _____

C Draw a picture to go with one of your sentences. Discuss your picture with a partner using the pronoun in the sentence.

Name _____

Action Verbs

There are different kinds of **verbs**.
Some verbs show action:

Mom **found** our jump rope.
She **gave** it to us.

 A Underline the action verb in each sentence. Then choose one of the action verbs to use in your own sentence. Tell your sentence to a partner.

1. Al <u>brings</u> the jump rope.

2. Eli and Linda <u>hold</u> the rope.

3. They <u>twirl</u> the rope.

4. The other kids <u>count</u>.

5. Scott's dog <u>barks</u> at the children.

6. Today Al <u>jumps</u> 100 times!

7. Then Linda <u>takes</u> a turn.

8. Mother <u>waves</u> from the window.

9. The kids <u>laugh</u>.

B Here are some more action verbs. Fill in each blank with a verb from this box.

dive	hear	pop
roars	visit	eat

1. Paul and Ann _____*visit*_____ the zoo.

2. They _____*hear*_____ some lions.

3. One of the lions _____*roars*_____ at them.

4. The elephants _____*eat*_____ lots of peanuts.

5. The polar bears _____*dive*_____ into the pool.

6. Prairie dogs _____*pop*_____ out of their tunnels.

Write a sentence about the zoo. Use an action verb.

_____

_____

_____

Name

Action and Linking Verbs

Action verbs show action. Here are some examples:

kick   tell   throw   ask   run   write

Linking verbs complete a thought or an idea. Here are some examples:

am   was   is   were   are   be

A | Write *A* if the underlined verb is an action verb. Write *L* if the verb is a linking verb.

___A___ **1.** Soccer players <u>kick</u> the ball.

___A___ **2.** Football players <u>throw</u> the ball.

___L___ **3.** I <u>am</u> cold.

___A___ **4.** Pat and Rob <u>run</u> around the track.

___L___ **5.** She <u>is</u> a fast runner.

___L___ **6.** They <u>are</u> both in second grade.

___A___ **7.** He <u>paints</u> pictures.

___L___ **8.** Pete and Joni <u>were</u> sick.

 **B** Pick five action verbs from the list on page 464 in *Write Source*. Use each action verb in a sentence.

1. _____

_____

2. _____

_____

3. _____

_____

4. _____

_____

5. _____

_____

 Write a sentence using the linking verb *am*.

_____

_____

Name _____

Verbs: Present and Past Tense

A verb that tells what is happening now is called a **present-tense verb**.

Sean **is** in second grade.
He **takes** swimming lessons every week.

A verb that tells what happened in the past is called a **past-tense verb**.

Last year he **was** in first grade.
He **learned** to play soccer.

 Check whether each underlined verb is in the present tense or the past tense.

	Present Tense	Past Tense
1. Bobby <u>broke</u> his leg last weekend.		✓
2. He <u>fell</u> out of a big tree.		✓
3. Now he <u>has</u> a cast on his leg.	✓	
4. He <u>is</u> home from school this week.	✓	
5. Yesterday I <u>took</u> him his homework.		✓
6. I <u>wrote</u> my name on his cast.		✓

138

B Complete the following sentences. Write the present-tense verb or the past-tense verb in the blank. The first one has been done for you.

Present Tense

1. Now Mom _____makes_____ my lunches for school.
(makes, made)

2. Now I _____am_____ eight years old.
(am, was)

3. The sidewalk _____gets_____ slippery when it snows.
(gets, got)

4. Now Stanis _____takes_____ swimming lessons.
(takes, took)

Past Tense

1. Last week I _____walked_____ to school with Hector.
(walk, walked)

2. Yesterday Lydia _____wrote_____ a letter to her aunt.
(write, wrote)

3. Last summer our family _____went_____ camping.
(goes, went)

4. This morning I _____was_____ late for school.
(am, was)

Name _____

Verbs: Present and Future Tense

A verb that tells what will happen in the future is called a **future-tense** verb.

We **will be** in third grade next year.

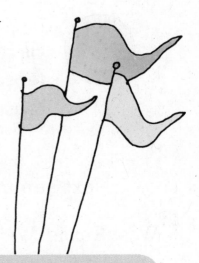

A Write the future tense for each verb. Then add two of your own examples. Tell a partner a sentence using one of the future-tense verbs.

1. climbed   _will climb_

2. make   will make

3. get   will get

4. carry   will carry

5. wanted   will want

6. play   will play

7. _____

8. _____

B Fill in the blanks by changing the present-tense word under the line into the future tense.

Next summer we ___will drive___ all the way across
 (drive)
West Texas. We ___will start___ in my hometown of Austin.
 (start)
We ___will take___ only the big highways. First, we
 (take)
___will stay___ overnight in Fort Stockton where Grandma
 (stay)
lives. Then we ___will wake___ up early the next day. We
 (wake)
___will keep___ driving until we reach El Paso, the western
 (keep)
tip of Texas.

Tell a partner what you will do over your next vacation. Use the future tense.

Name _____

Irregular Verbs

Irregular verbs do not follow the same rules as other verbs. They change in different ways.

	Present tense	Past tense
Example:	Birds **fly**.	Birds **flew**.

Study the irregular verbs in your textbook. Then complete the exercise below.

 Circle the correct verb in each sentence. Then tell a partner a sentence using one of the irregular verbs below.

1. My friend Kara (*rode,* *ridden*) a pony.

2. Uncle Billy (*came,* *come*) to visit us.

3. Last night, I (*sung,* *sang*) with my cousin.

4. Alfonso (*saw,* *seen*) a moose at the zoo.

5. Oscar (*done,* *did*) a good job on his art project.

6. The pitcher (*threw,* *throw*) the ball to first base.

142

In the sentences below, fill in the blank with the correct form of the verb shown. Then tell a partner sentences using the verbs _go_ and _went._

1. was   am

present: I ___am___ taking dance lessons.

past: I started dancing when I ___was___ four.

2. hide   hid

present: Sometimes, I ___hide___ from my dog.

past: Yesterday, I ___hid___ from him.

3. ran   run

present: We ___run___ with my big brother.

past: Last week, we ___ran___ at the track.

4. knew   know

present: I ___know___ Olivia.

past: When we met, I ___knew___ we would be friends.

Name _____

Adjectives 1

An **adjective** describes a noun or a pronoun. An adjective often comes before the word it describes.

Megan has long hair.
Randy wears a black cap.

Sometimes an **adjective** comes after the word it describes.

Parrots are colorful.

 A **Underline the adjective that describes each circled noun. Then tell a partner about an animal. Use at least two adjectives.**

1. Elephants are <u>huge</u> (animals.)

2. Their (skin) is <u>wrinkled</u>.

3. Their <u>ivory</u> (tusks) are <u>long</u> (teeth.)

4. Elephants use their <u>floppy</u> (ears) as <u>giant</u> (fans.)

5. An elephant's trunk works as a <u>useful</u> (tool.)

6. It can pick up <u>small</u> (peanuts.)

7. A <u>cool</u> (river) is an elephant's <u>favorite</u> (place.)

B Fill in each blank with an adjective that describes the circled noun.

(Answers will vary.)

1. Elephants make _____ (noises.)

2. Elephants have _____ (trunks.)

3. They have _____ (feet.)

4. Elephants can carry _____ (loads.)

5. Would you take a _____ (ride) on an elephant?

6. How would you get on a _____ (elephant?)

C Underline each adjective that describes the circled pronoun. Then tell a partner a sentence using the adjective *silly*.

1. (You) are <u>smart</u>.

2. (He) is <u>funny</u>.

3. (They) look <u>tired</u>.

4. (I) am <u>hungry</u>.

5. (It) is <u>green</u>.

6. (We) are <u>cold</u>.

7. (She) feels <u>sick</u>.

8. (They) taste <u>stale</u>.

Name _____

Adjectives 2

An **adjective** describes a noun or a pronoun. An adjective often comes before the word it describes.

The **hungry** bear sniffed the berries.

Sometimes an **adjective** comes after the word it describes.

The bear was **hungry**.

 A Underline the adjectives in this story. There are 12 in all. (Don't underline *a* or *that*.) Then add a sentence to the story using adjectives. Tell your sentence to a partner.

Once there was a little brown bear.

In the cool forest, she ate crunchy roots and red berries.

On summer days, the bear ate and ate.

In the fall, little bear changed.

She was a great, big bear.

She crawled into a cozy den for a long winter nap.

Write one more sentence for the story about the little bear. Underline the adjectives you use.

_____

_____

 **Write two sentences using adjectives from the box below. Try using more than one adjective in your sentences. Then choose another adjective from the box and speak using it in a sentence.**

hairy	purple	loud	cold
windy	wet	sweet	soft
chewy	sleepy	strong	sour

1. _____

_____

2. _____

_____

Name _____

Articles

The words *a*, *an*, and *the* are
articles.

Use *a* before a consonant sound.

➚ a kite

Use *an* before a vowel sound.

➚ an ocean

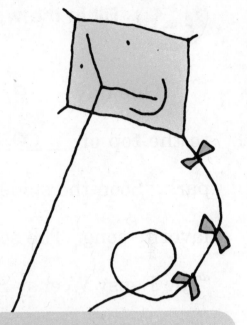

A **Write *a* or *an* before the following words. Then tell a sentence a partner using *a* or *an*.**

_an_	**1.** attic	_a_	**9.** whale
_a_	**2.** chicken	_a_	**10.** shadow
_a_	**3.** shovel	_an_	**11.** envelope
_an_	**4.** elephant	_an_	**12.** idea
_a_	**5.** tooth	_a_	**13.** monkey
_a_	**6.** giant	_an_	**14.** orange
_a_	**7.** dinosaur	_a_	**15.** package
_an_	**8.** apple	_a_	**16.** kettle

148

B **Fill in the word *a* or *an* in the spaces below.**

One day ___*a*___ spider with yellow feet climbed

to the top of ___*a*___ slide. The slide was in ___*a*___

park. Soon the spider heard ___*a*___ radio playing her

favorite song. The song was ___*an*___ old tune called

"The Eensy Weensy Spider." The spider began to tap her

eight yellow feet. ___*An*___ inchworm heard the music,

too. He inched his way over to the slide and began to tap

all of his feet. What ___*a*___ funny sight to see!

___*A*___ spider and ___*an*___ inchworm were dancing in

the park.

KEEP GOING

Draw a picture of the spider and the inchworm. Discuss your picture with a partner using the words *a* or *an*.

Name _____

Adjectives That Compare

Adjectives use different word endings to make comparisons. The ending *-er* compares two people, places or things. The ending *-est* compares three or more.

Compare **two**:

My brother's room is small**er** than my room.

Compare **three or more**:

The baby's room is the small**est** room in our house.

A Fill in each blank with the correct form of the adjective. Then tell a partner three sentences using the words *easier* and *easiest*.

longer, longest

1. A boa is ___longer___ than a grass snake.

2. A python is the ___longest___ snake in the zoo.

funnier, funniest

1. Leah's riddle was ___funnier___ than Garrett's riddle.

2. Ty's riddle was the ___funniest___ one in class.

Circle the adjective that compares two people, places, or things. Underline the adjective that compares three or more.

1. Kenny is the <u>tallest</u> player on the team.

2. Silver Lake is ⬭deeper⬯ than Cross Creek.

 Write one sentence using the adjective below. Then, tell a partner another sentence using the adjective *happiest*.

bigger

(Answers will vary.)

_____

_____

Name _____

Adverbs 1

An **adverb** is a word that describes a verb. It tells *when*, *where*, or *how* an action is done.

Some adverbs tell **when**:
yesterday   soon   always   early

Some adverbs tell **where**:
here   inside   up   below

Some adverbs tell **how**:
quietly   carefully   loudly   quickly

A In each sentence below, circle the adverb that tells *when*. Then tell a partner a sentence using a *when* adverb.

1. Aldo has (never) seen snow.

2. We woke up (early) so we could go fishing.

3. (Tomorrow,) our class is going to the museum.

4. Salma (always) wears her hair in braids.

B In each sentence below, fill in the blank with an adverb that tells *where*.

(Answers will vary.)

1. Our teacher will be _____ tomorrow.

2. Do you want to play _____ this afternoon?

3. I saw a mouse run _____ the stairs!

C Fill in each blank with an adverb from the box below. These adverb tells *how*.

(Answers will vary.)

gently	quickly	softly	cheerfully

1. Alexis smiled _cheerfully_ when she won the race.

2. "Have you seen Cory?" I asked _softly_.

3. Malik danced _quickly_ as he sang.

4. I rocked my baby sister _gently_.

KEEP GOING Tell a partner about a great day you had using when, where, and how adverbs.

Name _____

Adverbs 2

An **adverb** is a word that describes a verb. It tells *when*, *where*, or *how* an action is done.

Some adverbs tell **when**:
    finally   tomorrow

Some adverbs tell **where**:
    under   over

Some adverbs tell **how**:
    slowly   softly

 A   **Use adverbs to fill in each list below.**

When	Where	How
1. yesterday	1. _____	1. _____
2. _____	2. _____	2. _____
3. _____	3. _____	3. _____

 B   **Use your lists to tell a partner about a time you tried something new.**

C Fill in each blank with an adverb from the box.

quickly	carefully	in
quietly	often	under

1. Animals in the woods are _____ *often* _____ busy.

2. Squirrels look for acorns _____ *under* _____ fallen

leaves.

3. Deer _____ *quietly* _____ munch on weeds and grass.

4. Raccoons _____ *quickly* _____ open nuts for snacks.

5. Owls _____ *carefully* _____ watch for their prey.

6. Birds sing from high _____ *in* _____ the trees.

Choose two words from the box above. Use the words to tell a partner about an animal you have seen.

Name _____

Prepositions

A **preposition** is used to add information to a sentence.

Toby hit the ball **over** the fence.

Ally put a quarter **in** her bank.

Here are some common prepositions.

onto	up	with	at	of
before	below	like	in	to
as	over	down	along	on

A Circle the prepositions in the paragraph below. The chart above will help you. Tell a partner what happens to Troy next using prepositions.

1. Troy left camp (before) breakfast. 2. He pushed his bike (to) the top (of) the hill. 3. Soon, he was racing (down) it. 4. The wind rushed (through) his hair. 5. The bike's wheels bumped (along) the grassy path. 6. "Woo-hoo!" Troy shouted (with) joy.

Use the prepositions in this box to complete the following sentences. You will use one of the prepositions twice.

like	of	in	above	until

1. Beluga whales live ____in____ cold, Arctic waters.

2. Belugas are gray ____until____ they become adults.

3. Then they turn white ____like____ their parents.

4. They are often called "sea canaries" because ____of____ their songs and chatter.

5. Belugas swim ____in____ groups called pods.

6. Their sounds can be heard ____above____ the water.

 Tell a partner a sentence using a preposition from the box above.

Name _____

Prepositions and Prepositional Phrases

A **preposition** is used to add information to a sentence.

I live **in** a blue house.

A **prepositional phrase** begins with a preposition.

I live **in a blue house.**

 A Underline the prepositional phrases. Remember that they start with a preposition. Then use prepositional phrases to tell a partner how to get to your house.

1. It's easy to get <u>to my house.</u>

2. First, go <u>toward the high school.</u>

3. Then go <u>over that new bridge.</u>

4. Next go straight <u>up a steep hill.</u>

5. My house is <u>near the post office.</u>

6. There it is <u>between two tan houses.</u>

7. You will find me <u>inside the blue house!</u>

B Choose a preposition to begin each prepositional phrase.

behind	onto	around	on
with	for	after	in

1. Do something nice _____ for _____ your dog.

2. Give your dog a bath _____ in _____ the tub.

3. Sprinkle water _____ onto _____ your dog's fur.

4. Rub soap _____ on _____ the wet fur to make suds.

5. Wash all _____ around _____ the dog's body.

6. Don't forget to wash _____ behind _____ your dog's

   ears.

7. Gently dry your dog _____ with _____ a towel.

8. Give your dog lots of love _____ after _____ the bath.

Use prepositional phrases to tell a partner how you clean your bedroom.

159

 Write a preposition to begin each prepositional phrase.

1. We have fun playing any time _____ the year.

2. Most often we play _____ the playground.

3. In spring, we fly kites up _____ the hill.

4. In the summer, we swim _____ the lake.

5. Sometimes we read books _____ a tree.

6. During the fall, we rake leaves _____ the yard.

7. When its cold in winter, we play _____ the house.

8. Mostly, we just like to play _____ our friends.

 **Tell a partner what you enjoy doing in each season. Use prepositional phrases.**

160

Name _____

Conjunctions

A **conjunction** connects words or groups of words. The words *and* and *but* are the most common conjunctions.

Ramon writes poems **and** sings songs.

I was on time, **but** Tom wasn't there.

 Write one sentence using the conjunction *and*.

_____

_____

 Write one sentence using the conjunction *but*.

_____

_____

Two other conjunctions that connect words or groups of words are *or* and *so*.

Is Todd **or** Jaimee ready to bat?

It looked like rain, **so** she brought an umbrella.

C Circle the seven conjunctions in the story below.

The Tortoise (and) the Hare

Who won the race, the tortoise (or) the hare? They started out together, (but) the hare was much faster. He was way ahead of the tortoise, (so) he took a nap. The hare was snoring (and) dreaming when the tortoise walked by. Soon, the hare woke up, (and) he was amazed at what he saw. The tortoise was near the finish line! The hare ran to catch up, (but) it was too late. The tortoise won the race.

D Write a sentence using the conjunction *or*.

_____

162

Name _____

Interjections

An **interjection** shows excitement.
Some common interjections are:

Wow!   Yum!   Help!

Ouch!   Oops!   Hey!

 Write interjections to complete these sentences.

(Answers will vary.)

1. _____ ! This soup tastes delicious.

2. _____ ! I dropped my slice of pizza.

3. _____ ! I'm falling off the swing.

 Write a sentence using one of the interjections from above.

(Answers will vary.)

_____

_____

Draw a picture for each sentence below. Label each picture with an interjection.

(Answers will vary.)

_____
(interjection)

Look what I can do.

_____
(interjection)

That bug is huge.

_____
(interjection)

I pinched my finger!

_____
(interjection)

I dropped my lunch tray.

Name _____

Parts of Speech Review 1

In this activity, you will review the parts of speech you have practiced: **noun (N)**, **pronoun (P)**, **verb (V)**, and **adjective (A)**.

 What part of speech is underlined in each sentence? Write *N*, *P*, *V*, or *A* in the blank.

_A_ **1.** I like <u>toasted</u> cheese sandwiches.

_V_ **2.** They <u>smell</u> buttery and <u>look</u> golden brown.

_V_ **3.** When I <u>bite</u> into one, I <u>see</u> the melted cheese.

_N_ **4.** Toasted cheese <u>sandwiches</u> taste crunchy on the outside and creamy in the middle.

_P_ **5.** <u>My</u> mom makes them on the griddle.

_P_ **6.** <u>I</u> could eat one every day!

_N_ **7.** I hope we have toasted cheese sandwiches for <u>dinner</u> tonight.

_A_ **8.** It would be a <u>super</u> way to end my day.

B Fill in the blanks below.

1. Write the name of your favorite food (noun):

_____

2. Write a word that describes it (adjective):

_____

C Fill in each blank with a word that is the correct part of speech.

1. _____ likes tuna sandwiches.
(noun)

2. _____ like tacos better.
(pronoun)

3. I _____ two tacos every day.
(verb)

4. I like them with _____ cheese.
(adjective)

5. Sandra's mom _____ the best tacos.
(verb)

6. She puts _____ sauce on them.
(adjective)

166

Name

_____

Parts of Speech Review 2

 A Use the adjectives and adverbs in the box below to fill in the blanks in the sentences. Use each word only once.

small	smaller	smallest	tallest
exciting	large	wild	

1. Our zoo is an ___exciting___ place to visit.

2. Many ___wild___ animals live there.

3. Some are ___large___ and others are ___small___.

4. The giraffe is the zoo's ___tallest___ animal.

5. Otters and beavers are ___smaller___ animals.

6. Chipmunks are the ___smallest___ animals at the zoo.

Underline the prepositions in these sentences.

1. One cat rested <u>on</u> the desktop.

2. Another cat hid <u>inside</u> a drawer.

3. It hid <u>under</u> some papers.

 Use a comma and a conjunction to combine these short sentences. Use *or*, *and*, or *but*.

1. Should we play inside? Should we play outside?

_____

2. We went to the park. We had a picnic.

_____

 Write a sentence. Use one of the interjections below.

Wow!   **Yippee!**   **Help!**

_____

_____

168

Name _____

Parts of Speech
Review 3

 A **Choose the adverb that makes the most sense in each sentence.**

1. Parrots squawk _____loudly_____ in the treetops.
   (loudly, calmly)

2. Monkeys swing _____easily_____ through the branches.
   (easily, sadly)

3. Cheetahs run _____quickly_____ behind their prey.
   (softly, quickly)

4. Elephants walk _____heavily_____ across the plain.
   (heavily, gently)

5. Alligators slide _____smoothly_____ into the river.
   (smoothly, gladly)

6. Snakes slither _____quietly_____ through the grass.
   (quietly, wildly)

 B **Underline each prepositional phrase in the sentences above.**